OUR UNIVERSE

PLANET EARTH

Stephanie Warren Drimmer

Children's Press®
An Imprint of Scholastic Inc.

Content Consultant
Hsiang Yi Karen Yang, PhD
Assistant Professor
Institute of Astronomy
National Tsing Hua University
Hsinchu, Taiwan R.O.C.
(Former Computational Astrophysicist and Assistant Research Scientist in the
Department of Astronomy at the University of Maryland, College Park)

Library of Congress Cataloging-in-Publication Data
Name: Drimmer, Stephanie Warren, author.
Title: Planet Earth / Stephanie Warren Drimmer.
Other titles: True book.
Description: New York : Children's Press, an imprint of Scholastic Inc., 2021. | Series: A true book | Includes
    index. | Audience: Ages 8-10. |Audience: Grades 4-6. | Summary: "Book introduces the reader to Planet
    Earth"— Provided by publisher.
Identifiers: LCCN 2020004598 | ISBN 9780531132180 (library binding) | ISBN 9780531132364 (paperback)
Subjects: LCSH: Earth (Planet)—Juvenile literature.
Classification: LCC QB631.4 .D75 2021 | DDC 525--dc23
LC record available at https://lccn.loc.gov/2020004598

Design by Kathleen Petelinsek
Editorial development by Priyanka Lamichhane

All rights reserved. Published in 2021 by Children's Press, an imprint of Scholastic Inc.
Printed in Heshan, China   62

SCHOLASTIC, CHILDREN'S PRESS, A TRUE BOOK™, and associated logos are trademarks and/or
registered trademarks of Scholastic Inc.

Scholastic Inc., 557 Broadway, New York, NY 10012

1 2 3 4 5 6 7 8 9 10 R 30 29 28 27 26 25 24 23 22 21

Front cover: Earth appears as a giant blue marble from space.

Back cover: This poison dart frog is found in the tropical rainforests of Peru, South America.

Find the Truth!

Everything you are about to read is true *except* for one of the sentences on this page.

Which one is **TRUE**?

T or F About 70 percent of Earth's surface is covered by water.

T or F Hurricanes happen when cold, dry air over the Atlantic Ocean or Pacific Ocean begins to spin.

Find the answers in this book.

Contents

Emperor penguins

The **BIG** Truth

Are There Other Habitable Planets?

Newly discovered planet LHS 1140 b orbiting in front of its star.

4 Extreme Earth

How is climate change affecting Earth?

Introduction

Our Home Base in Space

The vast endless black of the universe holds **trillions and trillions of stars!** Stars move together in systems called galaxies. One of the **two trillion galaxies** in the universe is ours, **the Milky Way.** Its spinning spiral is made up of gas, dust, and billions of stars.

Countless numbers of those stars are not alone: They belong to solar systems, with planets that move around them. Our own solar system has eight planets. **The third planet from the sun is very special to us.** It is covered with blue oceans, green continents, and white puffy clouds. **It is our home: planet Earth.**

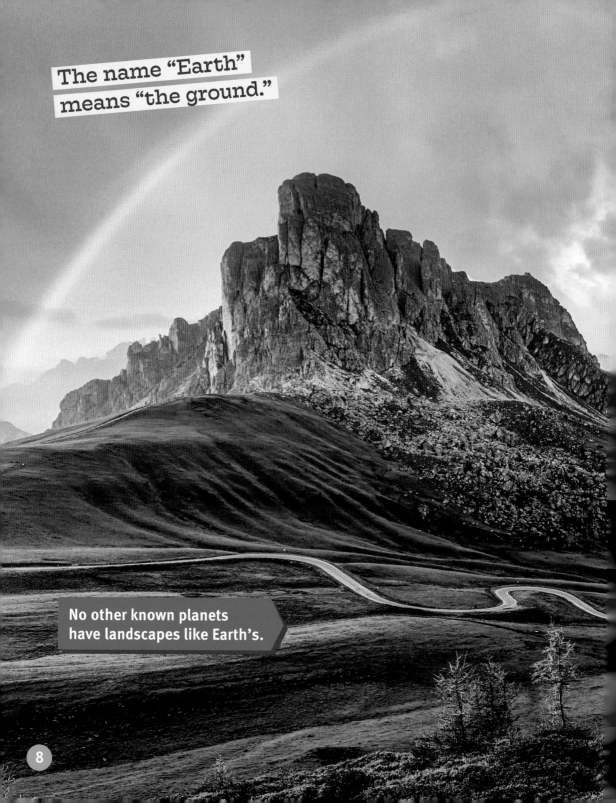

The name "Earth" means "the ground."

No other known planets have landscapes like Earth's.

Wondrous World

Earth is a planet unlike any other that we know. It has mountains and valleys, volcanoes and glaciers. Its surface is pelted by snowstorms and sizzled by lightning bolts. In all the universe, it is the only planet known to have an atmosphere with oxygen and oceans of liquid water on its surface. It is also the only place so far known to support life: plants and animals . . . and us!

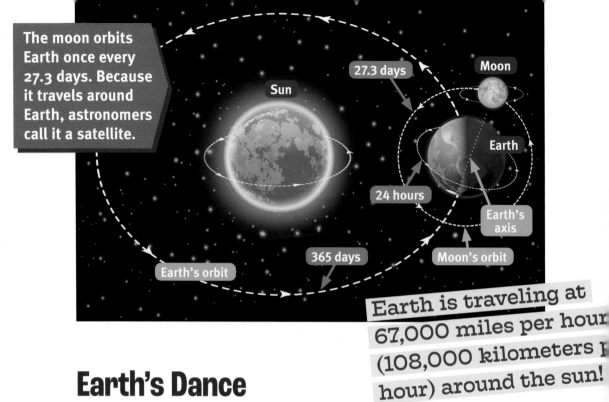

The moon orbits Earth once every 27.3 days. Because it travels around Earth, astronomers call it a satellite.

27.3 days

Moon

Sun

Earth

24 hours

Earth's axis

365 days

Moon's orbit

Earth's orbit

Earth is traveling at 67,000 miles per hour (108,000 kilometers per hour) around the sun!

Earth's Dance

You can't feel it, but Earth is moving under your feet. The planet spins, rotating around an imaginary line called an **axis**. It runs from the North Pole to the South Pole. Earth takes 24 hours to complete one full rotation on its axis: This rotation is what gives us day and night.

Earth also moves around the sun in an oval-shaped path, or orbit. It takes Earth 365 days to make one trip around the sun: This is what gives us our year.

The Seasons

Whether it's the chill of winter or the heat of summer, the seasons on Earth occur because our planet is tilted. Every year around June 21 in the Northern Hemisphere, summer begins. Earth is tipped so its northern half faces the sun. This creates warm temperatures and long days. During Earth's yearlong orbit, the seasons change as different areas of the planet are exposed to the sun's light and heat.

This graph shows Northern Hemisphere seasons. When it is winter in the Northern Hemisphere, it is summer in the Southern Hemisphere.

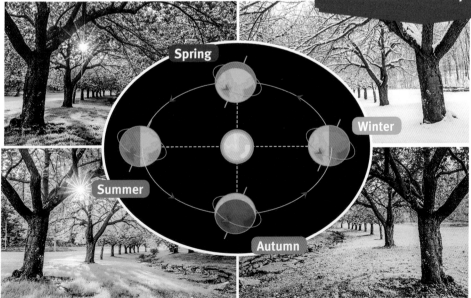

Spring

Winter

Summer

Autumn

Earth's Star

The sun warms our planet. But it does much more than that. Like other stars, the sun is an enormous ball of glowing gases. Its surface is about 10,000 degrees Fahrenheit (5,500 degrees Celsius)! Its gravity, or pulling force, is so strong that it holds the entire solar system together. The sun's heat affects our seasons, ocean currents, weather, and **climate**.

The sun is about 93 million miles (150 million km) from Earth.

If the sun were as tall as an average front doc Earth would be about the size of a nickel.

Meet the Neighbors

Earth is not alone in our solar system. Seven other planets also call it home. Here is a look at Earth and its neighbors in space.

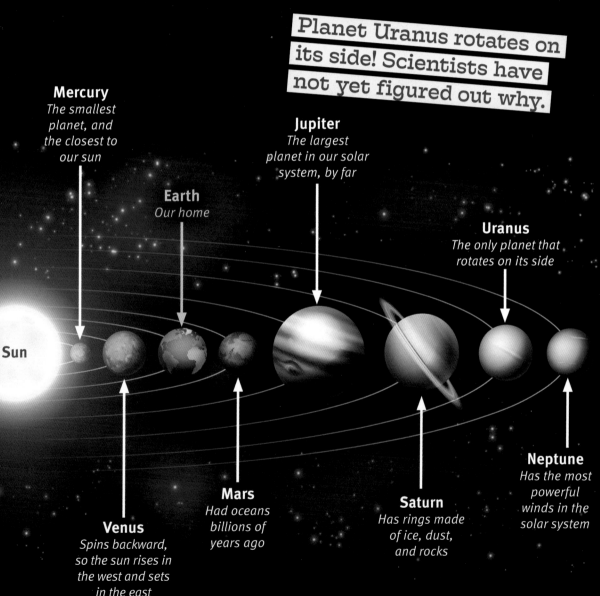

Planet Uranus rotates on its side! Scientists have not yet figured out why.

Mercury
The smallest planet, and the closest to our sun

Jupiter
The largest planet in our solar system, by far

Earth
Our home

Uranus
The only planet that rotates on its side

Sun

Neptune
Has the most powerful winds in the solar system

Venus
Spins backward, so the sun rises in the west and sets in the east

Mars
Had oceans billions of years ago

Saturn
Has rings made of ice, dust, and rocks

At more than 9,000°F (5,000°C), Earth's inner core is about as hot as the surface of the sun!

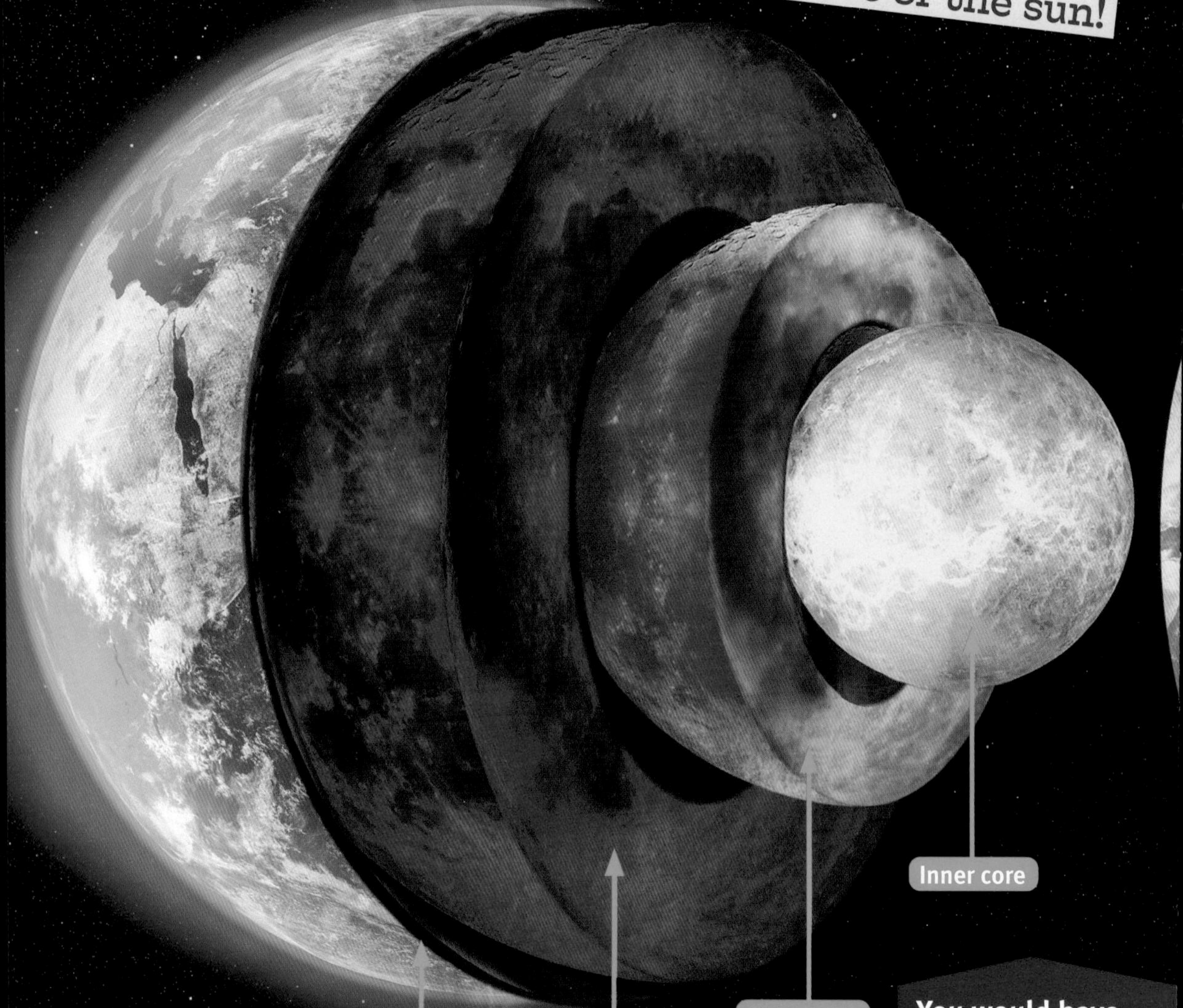

Inner core

Outer core

Crust

Mantle

You would have to tunnel almost 4,000 miles (6,437 km) to get to the center of Earth.

Understanding Earth

If you could dig far enough into Earth's surface, you would find that our planet has four different layers— the inner core, the outer core, the mantle, and the crust. As Earth formed, heavier materials sank toward the center and lighter ones rose toward the surface. Earth's inner core is made up of solid iron and nickel. The outer core is made up of hot liquid metals. The mantle is made up of rock that flows around slowly. Earth's crust is the thinnest layer. It is made up of solid rocks.

A Shifting Planet

Earth's crust is made up of plates that fit together like a jigsaw puzzle. These plates move about as fast as your fingernails grow, 1 to 2 inches (2.5 to 5 centimeters) per year. This process is called **plate tectonics**. And over millions of years, it has shaped Earth's surface into what it looks like today.

Timeline of Earth's Formation and Life on Earth

4.6 BILLION YEARS AGO (BYA)
Particles leftover from the sun's formation came together to form Earth. The other planets in our solar system also formed around the same time. Moons including Earth's moon, asteroids, and comets formed, too.

4 BYA
The continents started to form.

3.9 TO 3.8 BYA
Nobody knows exactly how life on Earth began, but many scientists think the first simple organisms came to be in the oceans.

Plate tectonics has pulled the continents apart and squashed them together. This has created Earth's surface features. In some places, the spreading of the plates has formed deep valleys. In other areas, the edges of plates grinding together have formed mountains and volcanoes. Millions of years of wind and flowing water on Earth's surface have reshaped these features even more.

65 MILLION YEARS AGO (MYA)
Plants became the first living things to take over the land.

240 MYA
The first mammals appeared.

65 MYA
The dinosaurs went extinct.

300,000 YEARS AGO
Humans appeared. They have made their way to every corner of the planet—and even outer space!

Water World

Earth is the only planet known so far to have liquid water on its surface. This is possible because Earth exists in the habitable zone. This is an area in space that is close enough to a star so that water does not freeze but far enough away so that water does not turn into steam.

About 70 percent of Earth's surface is covered by water. Most of this water is in the oceans. But water is also found underground, in the air as **water vapor**, and in rivers, lakes, and glaciers.

Only about 3 percent of Earth's water is freshwater.

Water is made of the elements hydrogen and oxygen.

The Water Cycle

Earth's water is always on the move. The water cycle is how it gets from place to place, all over our planet. This is how Earth's water cycle works.

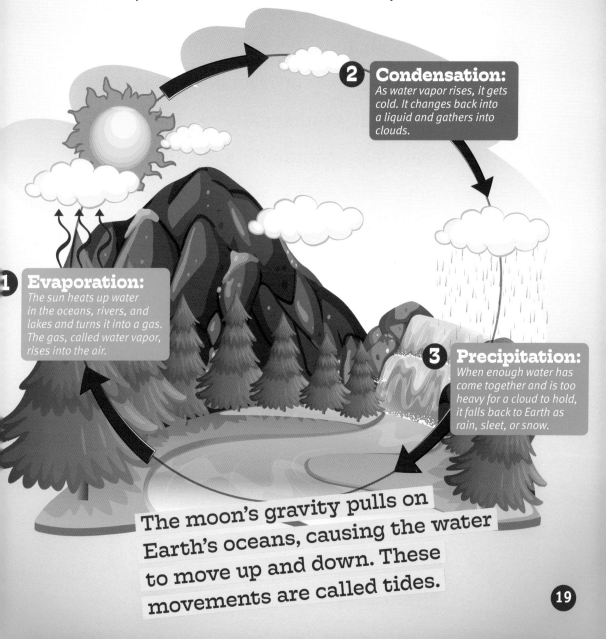

2 Condensation: *As water vapor rises, it gets cold. It changes back into a liquid and gathers into clouds.*

1 Evaporation: *The sun heats up water in the oceans, rivers, and lakes and turns it into a gas. The gas, called water vapor, rises into the air.*

3 Precipitation: *When enough water has come together and is too heavy for a cloud to hold, it falls back to Earth as rain, sleet, or snow.*

The moon's gravity pulls on Earth's oceans, causing the water to move up and down. These movements are called tides.

Ocean Planet

The oceans hold 97 percent of Earth's water. They are also where life began. Ocean water absorbs heat from the sun, and moves it around the globe on currents that act like conveyor belts. This process creates our weather patterns.

The oceans also contain lots of salt, and this salt comes from rocks. When rainwater hits rocks, the rocks slowly begin to break down. As this happens, salts are released into rivers and streams, which then carry those minerals into the oceans.

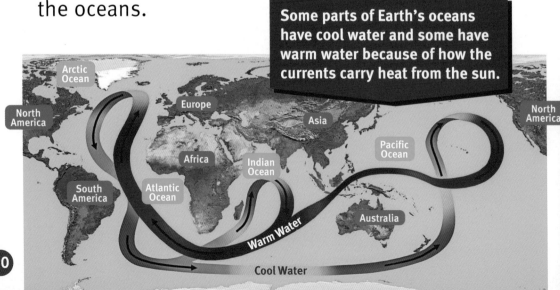

Some parts of Earth's oceans have cool water and some have warm water because of how the currents carry heat from the sun.

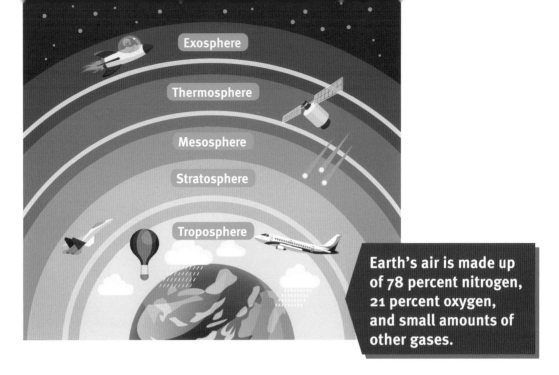

Exosphere

Thermosphere

Mesosphere

Stratosphere

Troposphere

Earth's air is made up of 78 percent nitrogen, 21 percent oxygen, and small amounts of other gases.

In the Air

Take a deep breath. *Ahhh*. You're inhaling Earth's atmosphere, the mixture of gases that surrounds our planet. The atmosphere not only gives us air to breathe but also keeps our planet warm and protects us from the sun's harmful radiation.

Earth's atmosphere is divided into layers. We live in the troposphere layer. This is also where clouds form. The exosphere is the outermost layer. It separates us from outer space.

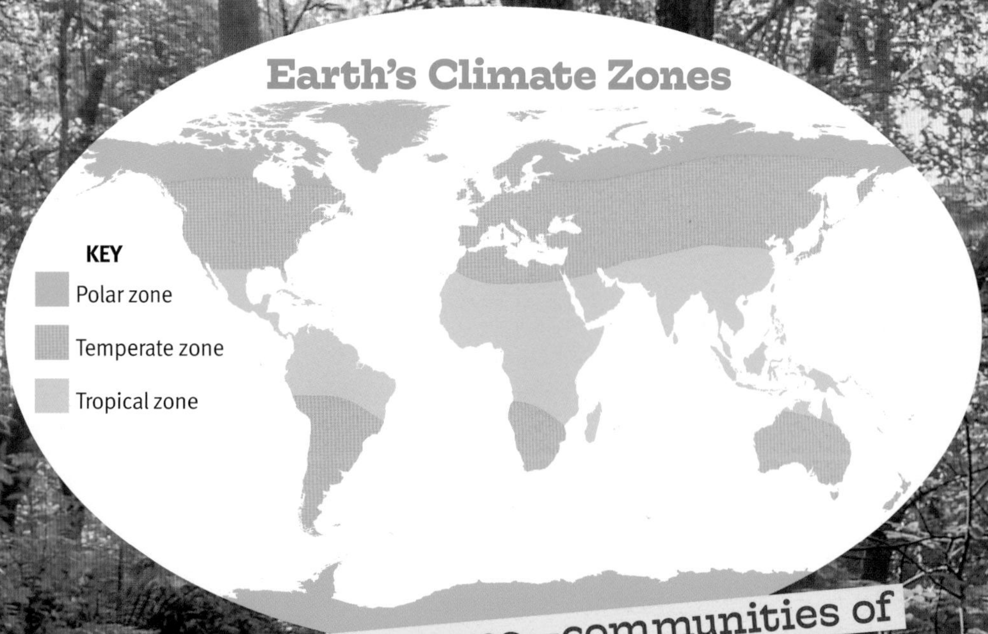

Earth's Climate Zones

KEY

Polar zone

Temperate zone

Tropical zone

Ecosystems—communities of living things that exist together in a specific area—are found in every climate in the world.

Rainforests are found in tropical climate zones. They cover less than 2 percent of Earth's surface, but are home to 50 percent of its plants and animals.

3

Living Earth

An unbelievable variety of living things make their home on Earth. There are about 390,000 plant **species** and eight million animal species on our planet. And an estimated one trillion species of tiny **microbes**!

Different creatures feel at home in different climates, even extreme ones. While many animals wouldn't survive long in the freezing Arctic, polar bears feel perfectly comfortable here. Our planet is divided into different climate zones. Each is home to its own plants and animals.

Tropical Zones

Better pack an umbrella! The tropical zones are known for their heat and dripping humidity. These areas are located near Earth's equator, where they are warmed by direct sunlight all year long. In some parts of the Amazon basin in South America, nearly 9 feet (3 meters) of rain falls every year!

All kinds of animals live in the tropical zones. Sloths and monkeys hang from trees. Boa constrictors slither along the ground, and colorful poison dart frogs hop from leaf to leaf.

There are more kinds of plants and animals in the tropical zones than anywhere else on Earth.

Poison dart frogs are some of the most toxic animals in the world.

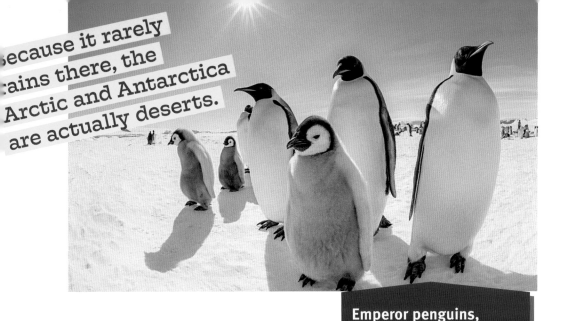

Because it rarely rains there, the Arctic and Antarctica are actually deserts.

Emperor penguins, shown here with their chicks, live in Antarctica.

Polar Zones

Brrr. Earth's polar zones are located at the very top and bottom of the planet, around the North and South Poles. Antarctica, around the South Pole, holds the record for the coldest temperature ever recorded on Earth, at -144°F (-97.8°C). In these frosty places, screaming winds and blowing snow can white out the landscape for days at a time.

Yet animals live here, too. In the Arctic, there are polar bears and narwhals. And in Antarctica, penguins and seals rule the ice.

Monarch butterflies migrate 3,000 miles (4,830 km) across North America.

Temperate Zones

In between the extremes of the tropical and polar zones lie the **temperate** zones. Here, the weather changes from season to season. Summers are warm, and winters are often snowy. Most of the United States, Europe, and Central Asia fall into these zones.

In the temperate zones, snowshoe hares change color with the changing seasons. And monarch butterflies migrate vast distances when summer changes to fall.

Underwater Zones

Earth's ocean is divided into zones, too. The top layer of the ocean is known as the sunlight zone. Lots of sunlight reaches this area, which is home to a variety of marine animals. Sea turtles, clownfish, and dolphins are found here.

Next is the twilight zone, where there is little sunlight. Lantern sharks and some jellyfish are found here. The deepest part of the ocean is the midnight zone, where there is no sunlight at all. Giant squid and anglerfish make their home here.

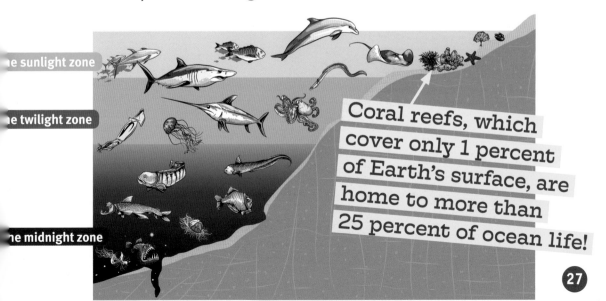

the sunlight zone

the twilight zone

the midnight zone

Coral reefs, which cover only 1 percent of Earth's surface, are home to more than 25 percent of ocean life!

Are There Other Habitable Planets?

The universe is full of planets—billions of them. Scientists believe it is likely that some of them are similar to Earth. These alien worlds could be home to their own plants, animals—and perhaps even intelligent beings like us. Scientists have already identified more than 4,000 exoplanets, planets outside our solar system that orbit a star. Here are the exoplanets most likely to support life.

There are an estimated one billion Earth-like planets in the Milky Way galaxy alone.

TRAPPIST-1 Planets

Location: The constellation Aquarius

It is believed that the seven planets orbiting the star TRAPPIST-1 are rocky worlds. All of them are about the size of Earth.

All images shown in The Big Truth are artist's conceptions.

Star LHS 1140

Planet LHS 1140 b

LHS 1140 b

Location: The constellation Cetus

This rocky planet is a "super-Earth" with a mass about seven times larger than Earth's.

Kepler-438 b

Location:
The constellation Lyra

This may be the most Earth-like planet ever discovered. Its average temperatures are similar to our planet's.

GJ 667 C c

Location: The constellation Scorpius

This planet may be in just the right spot to hold liquid water on its surface.

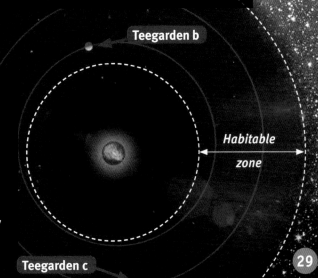

Teegarden b

Teegarden b and c

Location: The constellation Aries

These twin Earth-size exoplanets are just 12.5 **light-years** away from Earth.

Habitable zone

Teegarden c

Volcanic lightning forms in the column of ash released by some volcanoes.

Sakurajima volcano, shown here, is one of the most active volcanoes in Japan.

Extreme Earth

Earth is a very active place. It has extreme weather, including tornadoes and hurricanes that can blow away entire towns. Droughts and floods can dry up or drown large areas. These weather events are created when the sun heats Earth's surface.

The movement of Earth's tectonic plates is a force that shapes our planet's landscape. Tectonic plate movements can also cause earthquakes. Earth has a variety of extreme surface features, from volcanoes that spew red-hot lava to huge, icy glaciers.

Tornadoes and Hurricanes

Tornadoes form when rotating air is tilted vertically inside a thunderstorm. Some tornadoes can be more than 2 miles (3 km) wide. And their winds can reach speeds of more than 300 miles per hour (483 km per hour).

Hurricanes are the most powerful storms on the planet. They happen when warm, moist air over the ocean begins to spin. The storm becomes a hurricane when its winds reach speeds of more than 74 miles per hour (119 km per hour).

In the Southern Hemisphere hurricanes spin clockwise. In the Northern Hemisphere they spin counterclockwise.

In 2017, Hurricane Irma struck Miami, Florida, with winds over 100 miles per hour (161 km/hr).

Floods can leave entire neighborhoods underwater.

Droughts can dry out vegetation, creating fuel for wildfires.

Droughts and Floods

When there's not much rain, the ground can dry out and plants can die. When dry conditions last for weeks or years, the result can be a drought. A drought is a period of unusually dry weather that causes problems such as water and crop shortages.

Floods happen when water overflows into an area that is normally dry. Both heavy rainfall and melting snow can cause floods. Flash floods—floods that happen without warning—can be very dangerous for the people in their path.

Earthquakes can cause roads to collapse.

Earthquakes

Earthquakes can damage buildings and reshape Earth's surface. They happen when two tectonic plates suddenly slip past each other. These plates are always moving, but their edges are rough, which means they can get stuck. When the plates come loose, they release energy that causes the ground to shake.

Scientists can measure earthquakes using an instrument called a **seismograph**. But they can't predict when earthquakes will happen.

Tsunamis

A wall of water rises out of the sea and rushes onshore, wiping out everything in its path. It is a tsunami! These giant waves are usually caused by earthquakes on the seafloor. The biggest tsunami on record hit Lituya Bay, Alaska, in 1958. It was 1,720 feet (524 m) high—taller than the Empire State Building in New York City.

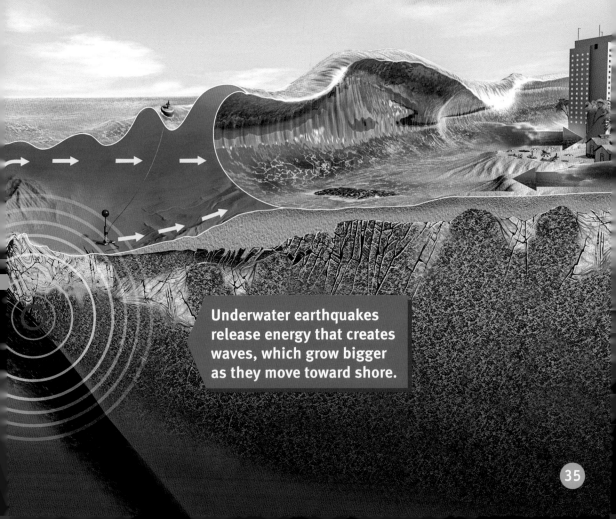

Underwater earthquakes release energy that creates waves, which grow bigger as they move toward shore.

Volcanoes

Like earthquakes, volcanoes occur where tectonic plates meet. This is where red-hot liquid rock called magma can rise up to the surface from Earth's mantle. When it explodes outward, it becomes lava. The result is a volcano.

Along with lava, volcanoes release a superhot mix of gases, ash, and rock. This can cause destruction for miles around. But volcanoes can also create new land: For example, the Hawaiian Islands were formed when lava from underwater eruptions hardened into rock.

Jupiter's moon Io has many active volcanoe'

Mount St. Helens in Washington erupted on May 18, 1980.

Chunks of ice break off a glacier in Alaska.

More than half of Earth's freshwater, about 69 percent, is held in glaciers and ice caps.

Glaciers

When snow falls over millions of years without melting, it can compress into a huge mass of ice. The ice becomes so heavy that it moves like a river, slowly flowing its way downhill. As it moves, it can carve valleys and reshape mountains. That's the power of a glacier.

Ten percent of Earth's land is currently covered by glaciers. But they're shrinking. Earth's glaciers are melting as the planet warms due to **climate change**.

Greenhouse gases make up only a small portion of the gases in our atmosphere. However, their effect has proven to be devastating.

Climate Crisis

Earth's climate has always been changing. But since the mid-20th century, it has been changing much faster than ever before. This is because humans burn fossil fuels, like coal, oil, and gas, for energy. Burning fossil fuels releases carbon dioxide and other **greenhouse gases** into the atmosphere. These gases act like a blanket, holding in the sun's heat and causing our planet to warm.

This process, known as climate change, has already caused Earth's average temperature to rise by about 1.8°F (1°C) since the 19th century. This rise could be causing more frequent severe weather events, such as droughts, floods, and hurricanes. And scientists think that if it continues, Earth's weather will become more extreme.

Warming temperatures threaten all life on our planet. It is important to protect Earth against climate change. It is our special home, and the only one we have, at least for now.

Millions of people around the world have taken to the streets to demand action on climate change from their governments.

A Warming World

To figure out how climate change is affecting Earth, scientists collect all kinds of information about our planet. Then they look for patterns. The maps on the right show information about the average July temperatures in the United States in 1895, 1935, 1975, and 2016. Study them, and then answer the questions.

Climate change can make weather even such as drought more extreme.

Average July Temperatures in the United States

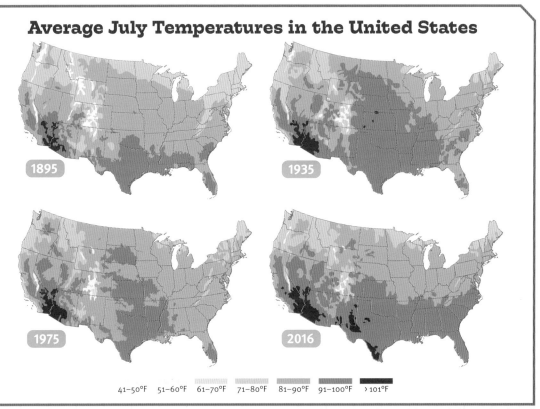

1895

1935

1975

2016

41–50°F 51–60°F 61–70°F 71–80°F 81–90°F 91–100°F > 101°F

Source: National Oceanic and Atmospheric Administration (NOAA)

Analyze It!

1 How many states had average temperatures above 90°F (32°C) in 1895?

2 How many states had average temperatures above 90°F (32°C) in 2016?

3 What patterns do you notice in the maps over time?

4 Think about what you've learned about climate change. Based on these graphs, how might a temperature map of July 2035 look?

ANSWERS: 1. 18. 2. 28. 3. The average maximum temperature in July in the United States is rising over time. 4. A map of July 2035 might have more dark red and dark orange spots than the map shown for 2016.

Tornado in a Bottle!

Planet Earth is home to incredible weather events—like tornadoes. Did you know you can make one right in your kitchen?

Materials

A clear plastic bottle with a cap

Water

Dishwashing liquid

Glitter

Directions

1 Fill the plastic bottle three-quarters full with water.

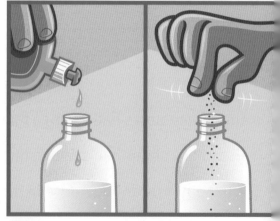

2 Add a few drops of dishwashing liquid. Then, add a few pinches of glitter to make your tornado easier to see.

3 Put the cap on. Make sure the bottle is tightly sealed!

4 Turn the bottle upside down. Holding the bottle by the neck, quickly spin it in a circular motion for a few seconds.

5 Stop and look inside the bottle. Can you see a mini tornado spinning there? If not, try again. It might take a few attempts to get it right.

Explain It!

Using what you learned in this book, can you explain what is happening to create the swirling tornado? If you need help, turn back to page 32 for more information.

True Statistics

Age of Earth: 4.6 billion years

Earth's distance from the sun: About 93,000,000 miles (150,000,000 km)

Amount of Earth's atmosphere that is made up of oxygen: 21 percent

Earth's largest continent: Asia

Earth's largest ocean: Pacific Ocean

Hottest recorded temperature on Earth: 134°F (56.7°C) in Death Valley, California (1913)

Coldest recorded temperature on Earth: -144°F (-97.8°C) in Antarctica (2018)

Earth's most active volcano: Kilauea volcano in Hawaii

Location of Earth's highest tides: Bay of Fundy, Canada

Did you find the truth?

(F) Hurricanes happen when cold, dry air over the Atlantic Ocean or Pacific Ocean begins to spin.

(T) About 70 percent of Earth's surface is covered by water.

Resources

Other books in this series:

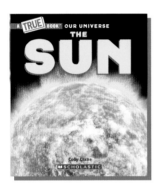  

You can also look at:

Macdonald, Fiona. *The Science of Oceans: The Watery Truth About 72 Percent of Our Planet's Surface*. New York: Franklin Watts, 2018.

Rathburn, Betsy. *Earth*. Minneapolis, MN: Bellwether Media, 2019.

Woolf, Alex. *The Science of Natural Disasters: The Devastating Truth About Volcanoes, Earthquakes, and Tsunamis*. New York: Children's Press, 2018.

Glossary

axis (AK-sis) an imaginary line through the middle of an object, around which that object spins, as in Earth's axis

climate (KLYE-mit) the weather typical of a place over a long period of time, as in a rainy climate

climate change (KLYE-mit chaynj) global warming and other changes in the weather and weather patterns that are happening because of human activity

greenhouse gases (GREEN-hous GAS-ez) gases such as carbon dioxide and methane that contribute to the greenhouse effect. These gases trap heat from the sun, which causes Earth's air and surface to warm.

light-years (LITE-yeerz) the distance that light travels in one year

microbes (MYE-krobez) extremely small living things

plate tectonics (playt tek-TAH-niks) the theory that Earth's crust is made up of huge sections, or "plates," that move slowly

seismograph (SIZE-muh-graf) an instrument that detects earthquakes and measures their power

species (SPEE-sheez) one of the groups into which animals and plants of the same genus are divided

temperate (TEM-pur-it) an area where the temperature is rarely very high or very low

water vapor (WAW-tur VAY-pur) water in gas form, which exists when water is heated above 212°F (100°C)

Index

Page numbers in **bold** indicate illustrations.

About the Author

Stephanie Warren Drimmer writes books and magazine stories for kids. Her work covers all kinds of science topics, from bugs to baby animals to the human brain. She has a master's degree in science journalism from New York University. She lives in Los Angeles, California.